# DO YOU WANT TO TALK ABOUT IT?

# DO YOU WANT
# TO TALK ABOUT IT?

## by Edward Koren

*Preface by Calvin Trillin*

PANTHEON BOOKS New York

*To the memory of my father*

Library of Congress Cataloging in Publication Data

Koren, Edward.
  Do You Want To Talk About It?

  Cartoons.
  1. American wit and humor, Pictorial. I. Title.
NC1429.K62A44      741.5'973      76-9988
ISBN: 0-394-73387-8
*Designed by Irva Mandelbaum*

Manufactured in the United States of America
First Paperback Edition

# Preface

I knew Ed Koren before his pen broke. I only wish I could remember precisely how he drew then. Imagine knowing El Greco before his astigmatism and not being able to remember whether his paintings in those days were filled with cuddly little fat people! Did Koren, before his weapon began missing like a Pontiac in need of new spark plugs, produce what the trade calls a "clean line"? (I realize that serious art historians might find it inappropriate that I compare Koren to El Greco—knowing, as they do, that Koren has never done a saint. On the other hand, even serious art historians must be looking forward to his first attempt.) I not only have difficulty remembering precisely how Koren drew in those days, I have difficulty remembering precisely how he looked. I know he didn't have a moustache then, but I find it hard to say whether the lack of facial hair made him look more or less shaggy. His personal appearance may seem to be a trivial matter (how many art historians, after all, dwell on the fact that El Greco was himself a cuddly little fat person?), but, as it happens, the question I am asked about Koren almost more than any other is whether he looks like the people in his drawings—"shaggy" being the adjective most used to describe them, although "hairy" is also mentioned regularly. The question asked even more often than that by people curious about Koren is whether he could draw a regular non-shaggy person or a regular non-hairy animal if he really tried. I always tell them that, as far as I know, he is trying as hard as he can.

There are people, of course, who believe that the condition of Koren's pen is not the secret of his success, just as there are people who believe that El Greco could see perfectly well except for the small print in the phone book. I have heard the rumor, still unverified, that an envious graduate student at Brown University—where Koren, presumably against his better instincts, taught Art for several years—stole Koren's pen after class one day, rushed to a drawing board in anticipation of producing a leering animal or a shaggy intellectual, and was able to turn out only a totally representational and extremely pedestrian portrait of the late John Foster Dulles. I realize that no less an authority than Hilton Kramer, the art critic of the *New York Times*, has implied in public print that Koren draws the way he draws on purpose. In a review of *The New Yorker Album of Drawings*, Kramer wrote, "Out of the unkempt hair styles and ragamuffin dress of the sixties, Mr. Koren has distilled a marvelously ironic comedy of manners...." On the other hand, another artist identified with *The New Yorker* has been heard to say that his usual response to seeing a Koren drawing is to start itching all over—presumably an effect Koren would not produce intentionally, considering his reputation for thoughtfulness toward colleagues. Still another artist whose work appears in *The New Yorker* once described Koren's drawings as resembling "the barbershop floor just before sweeping-up time." He said that rather approvingly, though, as if it were normal for a sophisticated habitué of uptown art galleries to stand before some highly acclaimed new painting and comment to his companion, "It does have a marvelous barbershop-floor quality to it."

"With Mr. Koren's cartoons, we are already laughing at the drawing before we even get to the captions," Kramer pointed out, and, as it happens, Koren's captions have been growing shorter as his line grows more hirsute. When the word got around that Koren himself was about to display some pictures on the wall of a posh uptown gallery, there must have been people who assumed that he had merely found a way to market drawings for which he could think of no caption at all. Not so. Koren's magazine work differs from what I believe scholars would classify as his Fine Art or Uptown Stuff in that the magazine drawings often leave some doubt as to which animal Koren had in mind, while the Uptown Stuff makes it difficult to tell whether what he had in mind was, in fact, an animal. The attempts by visitors to identify some of Koren's thing-like creatures we have hanging in the hallway of our house have been so varied that they call to mind the inspired Woody Allen description of watching a mime who was "either blowing glass or tattooing the student body of Northwestern University."

Koren's Uptown Stuff can also be distinguished from his magazine work in that it is manifestly for sale. Up to now, Koren has refused to sell the originals of his magazine drawings, leaving me no alternative except to maneuver myself into a position to receive them as gifts. As must have become clear by now, I am a great admirer of Koren's work, and I believe shameless acquisitiveness to be the sincerest form of flattery. Over the years, I have devoted almost as much energy to schemes for prying drawings from Koren as he has devoted to drawing them. I have suggested cartoon ideas to him on the assumption that the cartoon will be turned down by *The New Yorker*—an assumption based on my having compiled a lifetime cartoon turn-down record of one hundred percent—and that giving me the rejected drawing will strike Koren as the only decent thing to do under the circumstances. Once, while Koren was sitting with our family awaiting breakfast at a motel coffee shop in New Mexico, I encouraged my daughter Abigail, then three, to create a display of impatience so nerve-wracking that Koren had no recourse except to entertain her by drawing animals; the results, snatched up by me at the end of the meal while Koren was dealing with the check, turned out to be not only fine examples of Koren beasts but a testimony to the paper-preservation qualities of Holiday Inn placemats. Abigail is normally a charming rather than nerve-wracking little girl, and, like her younger sister, has proved useful in snuggling up to Koren and asking whether he happens to know how to draw a hippopotamus. He does, unless that was meant to be an antelope.

CALVIN TRILLIN
New York, 1976

*"We deal with it by talking about it."*

*"Dickie, I hardly recognized you! You've changed your format."*

*"We applaud excellence—regardless of the manner in which it manifests itself."*

*"Now tell us about your burglary."*

*"How's my sweet little bugaboo?"*

*"Young man, at table you either particularize or generalize, but not both."*

"Happy?"

"No more carbohydrates until you finish your protein."

*"Are you fully lined?"*

"You grew up in the fifties, didn't you?"

"We've decided not to have children."

"I work four hours in the morning. Then meditation and errands."

*"Anything you want at the store?"*

"Paul's got an article in the magazine section, Ann's book is reviewed by Dick, Buddy has a short piece on the Op-Ed page, Roy has something in the travel section, there's an essay by Norman on Matthew's new movie, and a letter on endangered species by your mother."

*"Note the densely distributed, yet perfectly balanced, relationship between the expressive line and the organic whole—how unity of surface is achieved by overtly lyrical variations of scale, texture, and color, giving three-dimensional form a spontaneous, plastically graphic definition."*

*"Do you want to talk about it?"*

*"Would you scratch my back?"*

*"We're planning a trip this summer to Area Codes 603, 802, and possibly 207."*

*"Yes, it __is__ beautiful, but will it serve eight?"*

*"Why such a long face?"*

*"Darling, let's get divorced."*

*"Just a little off the top and shape the back."*

*"I'd like everybody to meet Meg Plunkett, a wholly-owned subsidiary of Jack Plunkett."*

"Your bell sounds lovely this evening."

*"Is it too cutesy?"*

*"Bessie, it's them—the Bloomingdale couple."*

*"I __do__ think your problems are serious, Richard.*
*They're just not very interesting."*

"One, two, three. One, two, three. One, two, three..."

*"Really, Susan! I never thought of you as the hysterical type."*

*"Ah, Hopkins! <u>Finalmente!</u>"*

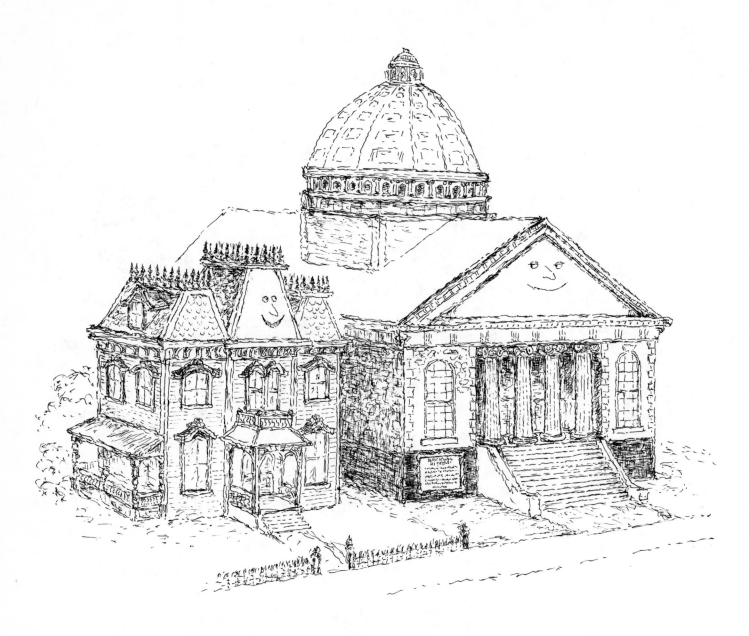

*"What did they give you—National Landmark or Historical Monument?"*

*"Wonderful seeing you!"*

*"You may be a sexist, but you're sweet."*

*"It's mighty good eating for the pennies it costs."*

*"I used to be a management consultant, but now I'm into making up songs and poems."*

"I don't feel like going out. Why don't just the two of us
stay in and open a can of worms?"

"They're leaving to be recycled."

*"One lyrical landscape—heavy on the Wyeth, light on the Expressionism."*

*"Good morning. I'm your Fuller Brush person."*

*"Air clean enough for you today?"*

"We were all wondering where you get your ideas."

"You've just raided your last patch!"

"A brilliant achievement...Unflinching...Writing at its most illuminating...
Gripping...Explosive...Long overdue...True vision...Plain speech...
Proclaims the failure of our civilization as a whole."

*"Loved the show!"*

*"What's it like to be at the top of the food chain?"*

*"He's just been given the nod from the New York Zoological Society."*

*"The sex isn't so much, but the violence is marvelous!"*

"We've re-struc-tured
   The fac-ul-ty stu-dent sen-ate, yeah man;
We've a-bol-ished
   R.O.T.C., ooh-ahhh;
There are eight-y fo-ur blacks
   In the fresh-man class, oh yeah…"

"Great news! 'Tarzan' is out in paperback!"

"This peak has never before been scaled by a group."

*"Well, back to the old grindstone."*

*"While I rather enjoy pistachio, almond fudge, and English-toffee twirl, I think my very favorite is still plain vanilla with sprinkles."*

*"While you were out for lunch, History passed by
and Fame came knocking."*

*"In a large bowl, combine 60¢ of eggs, 45¢ of medium cream, 16¢ of oregano, and 10¢ of dry mustard. Dip $7.50 of loin pork chops into this mixture and roll in 65¢ of bread crumbs. Heat 90¢ of peanut oil in a heavy skillet and slowly fry the chops on 94¢ of gas."*

*"I'd like you to meet Frank Russ. He's just arrived on foot."*

"I know I'm being paranoid, but I think we should be a little careful
about expressing ourselves too freely."

*"Have you given any thought to what you'll do with your Saturdays when the world's fossil fuels are used up?"*

*"He's one thousand years old today!"*

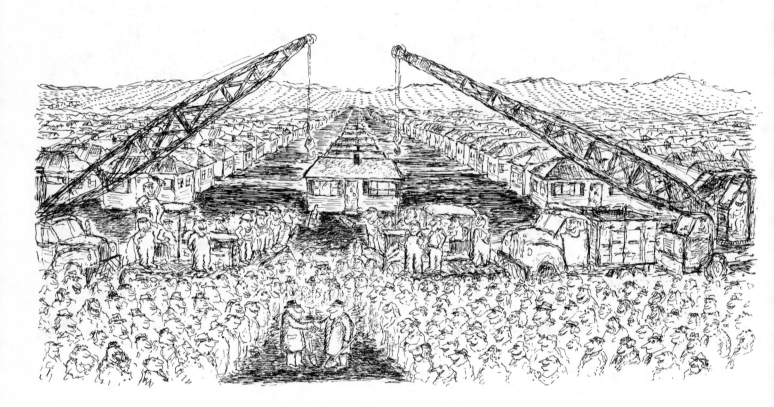

*"At last! One nation, indivisible."*

*"Could you tell us something about performance, design, engineering, workmanship, safety, and service?"*

*"And what salutation do you want to use with this letter, Mr. Dubbins?"*

*"What would you say the precipitation probability is for today?"*

"So let's have a big paw for a really great performer."

*"Be gentle with it, men. It's a historic landmark."*

*"You look disgustingly healthy."*

*"I just couldn't resist congratulating you boys. Your music has contributed enormously to the vitality of our culture."*

"Yes, I _am_ into a new thing, dear child. It's called embroidery."

*"May I join your rumination group?"*

"Tell me, sir. Is it good or bad?"

*"Broderick, what do you know about evolution?"*

*"There surely must be some mistake—I'm middle-class!"*

*"Well, there she goes—the 5:08 to Los Angeles. Right on time!"*

*"Quick! Get your gun, Pa! Here come the suburbs."*

*"Concept...generalization...articulation...conclusion!"*

*"They're part of our dwindling farm population."*

*"With this sculpture, the current crisis between the object and the image reaches into the more fundamental conflict between the metaphysical angst of the first-generation Abstract Expressionists and the space-environment preoccupations of the avant-garde."*

*"We all realize that violence should never take the place of reasoned discussion in the settlement of most disputes."*

*"April 20: The weather continues sunny and warm."*

"Tonight, we're going to let the statistics speak for themselves."

*"He's charged with expressing contempt for data-processing."*

*"I love to hold your wing in mine, to touch your
beak, to ruffle your plumes..."*

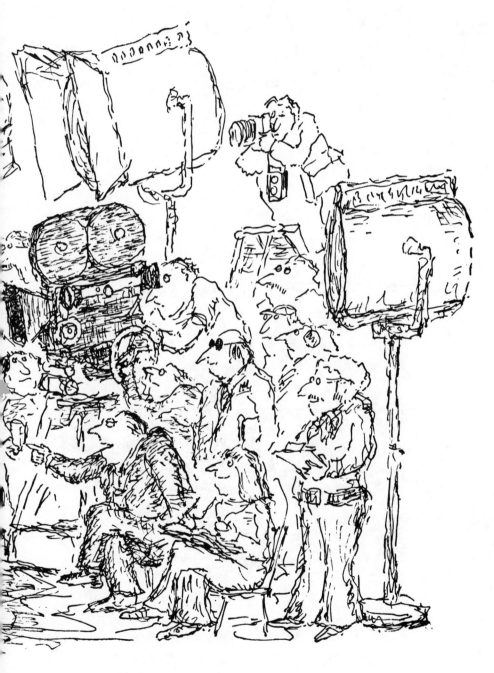

*"Lights! Camera! Love!"*

"I am calling from an antique phone, Operator, and I
want Information, not Directory Assistance."

"Zero population growth!"

"Martin and I just bought sixty-five acres in Vermont, and as soon as
we get around to building a house you must come up and visit."

*"Some of us long for the days of the old taboos."*

*"What we'd like is a four-hundred-thousand-word novel that oversteps the bounds of decency."*

*"You are an affront to the palate."*

*"Extend your left rear paw behind you. Raise your right front paw above your head and extend your left front paw straight in front of you. On the count of four, breathe deeply..."*

"Are you a hunter or a food gatherer?"

*"Next I want to sing a song about the House Rules Committee and how the legislative functions of Congress are tyrannized over by its procedural calendar, dominated in turn by an all-powerful chairman hamstringing the processes of democracy."*

*"Hugh just loves to drive."*

*"We found the most marvelous little place where they sell gasoline."*

*"They represent one hundred and nineteen years of experience."*

*"Oh dear! It <u>isn't</u> a boutique!"*

"Daddy! Daddy! American planes bombed a key rail depot near Hanoi
and knocked out a power station today in a record number of strikes
for the third consecutive day!"

"It looks as though Dean Smith is no longer beloved."

"Excuse me, but what's the nature of this bar? Political, literary, or singles?"

*"I'm sorry, but it just isn't working out between us, Jeffrey. You're
an orange, and I want an apple."*

"Our next mind-shattering song is a simple A—B—A form which relies on the rhythmic texture and variation of naive American marching music and Renaissance madrigals."

"I'm no stranger to the creative act myself."

*"French, Italian, Russian, or Thousand Island?"*

"You're suffering from sensory overload. Cut down on your intake of media."

"We've heard some wonderful things about you from Boojum!"

*"Tonight we're not saying anything unless it's significant."*

"A very effective dating service, I must say."

*"Well, now we've seen it."*